Some Observations

on

Eighteenth Century Poetry

Some Observations

on

Eighteenth Century Poetry

By

DAVID NICHOL SMITH

Merton Professor of English Literature in the
University of Oxford

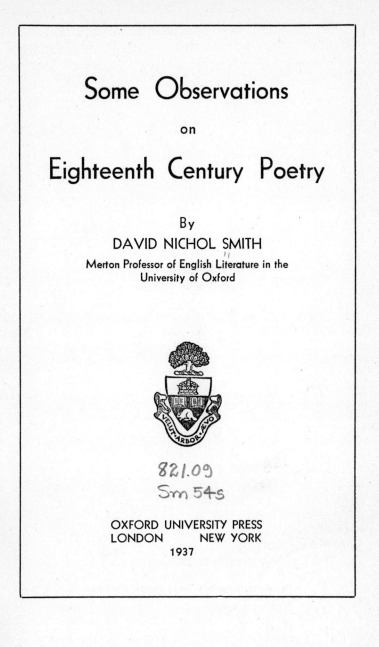

OXFORD UNIVERSITY PRESS
LONDON   NEW YORK
1937

PRINTED IN CANADA
BY
THE UNIVERSITY OF TORONTO PRESS

THE ALEXANDER LECTURES IN ENGLISH
AT
THE UNIVERSITY OF TORONTO
1937

THE ALEXANDER LECTURESHIP

THE Alexander Lectureship was founded in honour of Professor W. J. Alexander, Head of the Department of English Literature in University College from 1889 to 1926. The funds necessary for the purpose were collected by a large number of the old students and friends of Professor Alexander immediately after his retirement. The object of the lectureship is to bring to the University each year a distinguished critic, man of letters, or university professor, usually from another country, who will give a course of from three to six lectures on some subject related to English Literature. The lectures are published either by the lecturer himself or by the University of Toronto Press. The list of Alexander lecturers since 1929 is as follows: Professor Cazamian of the Sorbonne, Professor Garrod of Oxford, Professor Babbitt of Harvard, Sir William Craigie of Chicago, Professor Grierson of Edinburgh, Professor Sedgewick of British Columbia, Professor Stoll of Minnesota, Professor Snyder of Northwestern University, Professor Nichol Smith of Oxford.

London:
HUMPHREY MILFORD
Oxford University Press

———

New York:
OXFORD UNIVERSITY PRESS

I

POPE—POETIC DICTION

IN offering to speak to you about the poetry of
the eighteenth century I have in mind both
the opinion in which it has been generally held
since the days of Wordsworth and Coleridge, and
the growing disinclination to take that opinion on
trust. The confusion of our groping and crowded
times has aroused a new interest in the controlled
simplicity of that great body of poetry, so unlike
the poetry which these times are themselves pro-
ducing; and this new interest may be expected to
lead to a reassessment. All that I propose to do in
the three lectures which I have now to deliver
in honour of Professor Alexander is to make a
series of remarks on matters or aspects which of
late have been receiving attention and are likely
to be taken into yet fuller consideration.

Perhaps we are only now getting far enough
away from the eighteenth century to see its poetry
clearly and dispassionately. Somehow it moved
the passions of the nineteenth century, and what
some of us have been saying about the Victorians
is not more unkind and self-satisfied than what the
Victorians themselves said about their grand-
fathers. There should be no occasion now for
passion at the safe distance of two hundred years.
We have outlived it when we speak of the other

arts as practised in the eighteenth century. Its architecture and landscape gardening, its painting and music, whether or not they are liked, are now treated with becoming impartiality. But its poetry is only now reaching that happy stage; only now are we coming to think of it as an expression of the English genius at one of the great and characteristic periods of its history.

To a greater extent than most of us realize, we are, in matters of literary taste, the pupils of the nineteenth century. We may think that we have escaped from it, but oftener than we seem to know we are only repeating what it told us. When a man gets rid of all the Victorian furniture that he has inherited and fills his rooms with Chippendales or older pieces and at the same time expresses the familiar Victorian doctrine about Pope and Gray and Johnson, I confess that I am somewhat puzzled, and I wonder whether he holds his views on poetry from conviction. Even the most independent of us must take some things on trust, and the man who proclaims his independence in his politics, his religion, or his manners, may sometimes be found talking about poetry much as his father did, and his grandfather.

The call for the reopening of the case has come mainly from our universities,—not from all of them by any means, but from universities on both sides of the Atlantic, and from a greater number on this

side than on the other. I should like to take this
opportunity of expressing the opinion that Eng-
land can no longer claim a clear lead in eighteenth
century studies. It is true that most of the more
important publications are still printed in England.
But who are the authors or editors? Where were
the books written? Our great authority on the life
of Pope is now at Columbia University. The un-
approached authority on Horace Walpole is a
devoted son of Yale. Another son of Yale is the
first and final editor of most of the new Boswell
papers. Our most scholarly edition of the letters
of Burns has not been prepared in Scotland. I am
not thinking of the great bulk of the work on the
literature of the eighteenth century produced every
year, but only of the work that is of outstanding
importance. And it must be a very special
pleasure to us all that Toronto should take her
place in the forefront of this movement with the
admirable edition of *The Drapier's Letters* by my
old friend Mr. Herbert Davis.

First of all let me remind you of the continual
ebb and flow in the history of our literature. The
building up of a system is followed by its collapse.
Great men bring a particular type of poetry to its
highest achievement; they are copied; what was
an individual method of self-expression becomes a
convention; and once convention arises the men

who will break through it are not far off. This
process is well illustrated at the present day. The
younger poets are suspicious of what some of us
would call the tradition in English poetry; they
detect convention. We may not like their own
poetry; to some of us it is very difficult, and I
sometimes suspect very difficult to everyone except
the author; still, viewing it historically, we must
assume that it represents a stage, and that some-
thing larger and more definable will arise out of it.
But when that happens this poetry will itself
become conventionalized—indeed I suspect that
it already is becoming so—and for that very
reason may expect to be attacked. I would ask
you to remember this regular and inevitable pro-
cess when you consider the poetry of the eighteenth
century.

This poetry had itself arisen from the ruins
of an outworn convention. But let me go back
to Elizabethan times. Shakespeare did not fight
against convention. It was his habit to make the
best of what he found; and his genius so completely
triumphed over convention that we do not see it
in his work till we think about it. But Donne
would not accept it; he openly fought against it.
He tried to get closer to experience and to represent
it without the disguise of fashion. In his endeavour
to express what he felt he called his strong intel-
lectualism to his aid, and drew his similes from

unexpected quarters.   These similes and conceits
became a characteristic part of his poetry, and
they invited imitators who lacked his strength of
feeling and his controlling sense of experience.
Donne, who broke through one convention, was to
be unknowingly the creator of another.   The
metaphysical school which emerged was a great
school when under the direction of its masters.
But there are never many great masters in any
school, and the metaphysical school had many
members.   As the lesser men cultivated the con-
ceit for its own sake, or without due care of the
purpose which it ought to serve, the school de-
cayed.   The time came for order to be brought out
of chaos.   Again the cry was raised—get closer to
experience, return to Nature.

The great leader in this movement was Dryden.
His guiding motive, in so far as it can be briefly
stated, is to deal with life as he knows it, forcibly,
unmistakably, in language that can be at once
understood and is yet charged with meaning.   He
will not avoid similes and figures of speech—no
poet can avoid them for long—but he will not
seek for them nor introduce them for their own
sake; they must arise naturally out of what is being
said, just as they present themselves in ordinary
speech.   Be clever if you like, but beware of trying
to be cleverer than you really are, for that is the
sure way to be dull.   Do not use too many words.

If a man knows what he wants to say, the chances are,—if indeed he does know what he wants to say,—that he will express himself briefly and pointedly. Control the development of the thought; do not let it be said of you:

> He faggoted his notions as they fell,
> And if they rhymed and rattled, all was well.

In any case deal with life as it is known, and in such a way as will be readily understood. The poet does not write for a coterie, a privileged few who know his special point of view and are prepared to wrestle with his conundrums; the poet writes for the community.

These new aims in poetry were never better stated than by Dryden at the outset of his career, in his essay *Of Dramatic Poesy*: "Our poesy is improved by the happiness of some writers yet living, who first taught us to mould our thoughts into easy and significant words, to retrench the superfluities of expression, and to make our rhyme so properly a part of the verse, that it should never mislead the sense, but itself be led and governed by it." And again: "Wit is best conveyed to us in the most easy language, and is most to be admired when a great thought comes dressed in words so commonly received that it is understood by the meanest apprehensions, as the best meat is the most easily digested."

The leadership passes to Pope, and he is a loyal successor who, despite his strongly marked individuality, never falters in his admiration. He has the same ideals; the differences between his work and Dryden's do not spring from different aims. The older man is more robust and able to move with a greater swing; the younger is more delicate and takes greater care,—perhaps he is the greater artist. At the beginning of his career Pope made a deliberate statement of his poetical doctrine, his *Essay on Criticism*. It was not a casual statement such as Dryden had introduced, somewhat unexpectedly, into his essay *Of Dramatic Poesy*. I do not say that the *Essay on Criticism* is wholly satisfactory as an explanation of Pope's later practice. I doubt if any English poet has ever made a statement of his poetical theory that tallies at all points with his practice. But what Pope says in his *Essay on Criticism* is in as close agreement with the poetry of Dryden as with his own.

In the poetry of the first half of the eighteenth century Pope stands out by himself. He has no rival; but we must not therefore speak about the tyranny of Pope. There are no dictators in English poetry. Every poet is at liberty to write as best he can. Such influence as Pope exerted was only an acknowledgement of his quality. His excellence invited imitation; it established a fashion; but it also acted as a deterrent. His

supremacy in the heroic couplet was an incentive
to some younger poets to write in other measures.
I would ask you to remember that very few of the
greater poems of the eighteenth century, other
than Pope's, are written in the heroic couplet.
How many can we name offhand besides Johnson's
and Goldsmith's?   Thomson wrote in blank verse
and the Spenserian stanza, Collins wrote odes,
Gray wrote odes and is best known for his *Elegy*.
Should we desire a rapid ocular proof of the great
variety of measures employed by the poets of this
country, we cannot do better than turn the pages
of the miscellanies or anthologies which were then
in fashion, and best of all Dodsley's *Collection of
Poems by Several Hands*, the most famous and most
representative of them all.   The small proportion
of poems in the heroic couplet to be found in this
collection may come as a surprise.

The poets who wrote in the heroic couplet after
Pope had the music of his verse ringing in their
ears, and unless they were men of strong individu-
ality, who could make this difficult measure serve
their purpose, they were bound to echo his music
and reproduce his language. Again convention
had come.   A school which in its rise had rejected
an outworn convention had itself sunk into con-
vention of another kind.   It was time that Words-
worth and Coleridge should call for a return to
Nature, the same call which had been uttered, in

very different circumstances, by the founders of
the school which they were to displace. Every
new movement in English poetry proclaims the
return to Nature. I am told that our modern
poets believe that they are getting nearer to
Nature.

The truth is that upon Pope have been visited
the sins of his imitators, even two or three genera-
tions of them. Wordsworth and Coleridge had
good reason to attack the conventionalism of
English poetry when they were young men. But
what was conventionalism in Pope's self-elected
imitators is not conventionalism in Pope himself.

Ever since Wordsworth wrote his famous pref-
ace to *Lyrical Ballads* we have heard much, and
rightly, about the poetic diction of the eighteenth
century; and many who speak of it seem to forget
that the virtue of poetic diction at any time must
depend on the purpose and manner of its use.
A great poet may breathe new life into a worn-out
phrase. On the other hand, a phrase which pul-
sates in the dramas of Shakespeare may appear
vapid when introduced into poor verses. A Spen-
serian jewel may be a false ornament. What we
have always to consider is whether the poet has
succeeded in keeping his diction alive, whether it
serves an organic function, or whether it is a mere
decorative make-weight. We have also to remem-
ber that words change their meaning, and may

have associations to us which the older poets could not have suspected. The word "blushing", for instance, needs to be carefully used nowadays, and the word "gale" calls up a picture of havoc and shipwreck. In Pope's time "gale" was used much as we use "wind"; it might mean a "gentle breeze".

> Where'er you walk, cool gales shall fan the glade;
> Trees, where you sit, shall crowd into a shade;
> Where'er you tread, the blushing flowers shall rise,
> And all things flourish where you turn your eyes.

Someone may say: "Ah, poetic diction, 'cool gales', 'blushing flowers'." But are these words otiose? Are not these lines completely satisfying as an expression of what the poet means to convey? To many they are best known in the setting of Handel and I suspect that not everyone who is familiar with the music is aware that the words are by Pope. The beauty of the music has over-powered the gentler beauty of the words, and yet there are some who prefer the words.

Let me give another well-known illustration:

> Here where the mountains less'ning as they rise
> Lose the low vales, and steal into the skies:
> While lab'ring oxen, spent with toil and heat,
> In their loose traces from the field retreat;
> While curling smokes from village-tops are seen,
> And the fleet shades glide o'er the dusky green.

"Lab'ring oxen", "curling smokes", "fleet shades", "dusky green". But who will say that this care-

fully pencilled picture of an autumn evening in the
country fails to give us what the poet saw and
meant us to see?

These two passages occur in Pope's first
publication, his *Pastorals*,—remarkable prentice
work, and especially remarkable for the sustained
music of the smooth verse. He aimed at smooth-
ness, as he tells us, in these *Pastorals*, and he
attained it. He was soon to aim at other effects,
with equal success. But even as a boy he had
learned that the measure must be adapted to the
subject, that the instrument must be made respon-
sive to the poet's mood. The heroic couplet has
a way of controlling or limiting the poet, and very
few poets can do with it what they like. But
Pope had it under his control; and he proved that
it is an instrument of even wider range than
Dryden had shown.

His care for the right word never relaxes. He
is said by Johnson to have searched the pages of
Dryden for happy combinations of heroic diction.
With the same purpose he read Milton and Spenser.
He uses words that are enriched by their associa-
tion with his great predecessors; he indulges
deliberately in the conscious echo; he looks for the
word that he wants, as we all do, and he will take
it wherever he finds it; but what he takes he sub-
dues to his purpose. Far from his diction being
conventional, I believe that if we could go back to

Pope knowing only the poetry that had been written before his time and the poetry that was being written by his contemporaries, we should find in the allusiveness and the aptness of his diction the charm of novelty.

If only we could see Pope as Johnson saw him we should get nearer the truth on this debatable matter,—or rather, I am tempted to say, this matter on which there has been much misunderstanding. "He has left in his Homer", says Johnson, "a treasure of poetical elegances to posterity." It was a treasure that was rifled by his imitators who did not always establish their right to what they took. And so Coleridge could say that Pope's Homer was "the main source of our pseudo-poetic diction". When poetical elegances were adopted lazily, mechanically, there was good reason for condemnation. Phrases must lose their virtue as they become familiar; happy epithets degenerate into stock epithets. The poetic diction that Coleridge condemned is the second-hand word or phrase that has not been bettered in the borrowing. The borrowed jewels of Pope's imitators were too obviously borrowed.

Pope's Homer was written midway in his career. Having formed this "treasure of poetical elegances", he was to prove himself in his later work to be one of the great masters of the familiar style,—the style in which the poet uses the language of ordinary speech; and that is the language of satire and the friendly epistle. It was part of Wordsworth's reform, you will remember, to use what he calls "a selection of language really used by men". He aimed at getting rid of recognized poetical elegances; he denied that poetry has a language or a phraseology peculiar to itself. But there was less novelty in his views than he would have had his readers believe. Dryden, who also had reform in view, had spoken, as we have seen, of moulding our thoughts "into easy and significant words", and it was "a selection of language really used by men" that Pope used in his Satires and all his later work. I propose to take as representative of Pope's Satires the famous passage on Atticus, and I do so the more readily as it has often been misunderstood. In origin it was a satire on Addison, but as we now read it in the *Epistle to Arbuthnot* it is a satire on certain personal failings to which a great writer is sometimes liable. Pope intended it in its final form to represent the type, and not an individual.

But first let me point out that this is equally true of all the character-sketches to which Pope does not give a definite English name. There can be no doubt about his Man of Ross, and Villiers, and Duke of Wharton,—the name is written on the portrait. But much ink has been spilt on whom he meant by Bufo, and Atossa, and Timon. The portraits do not agree with all the known facts about the Earl of Halifax, and the Duchess of Marlborough, and the Duke of Chandos, and for this reason, that in drawing Bufo Pope meant to represent not a particular man but a literary patron, in Atossa an imperious woman, and in Timon a grand seigneur who lavished his money in the pursuit of taste.   Whenever a man describes a type he must draw his details from an individual, and he may draw them from several.   All our general ideas derive from particular instances; describe the genus dog, and we cannot escape from thinking of particular dogs that we have known. When Pope proceeds to describe the great literary patron, as a type, what he knew of the Earl of Halifax may well have occurred to him.   But if Bufo is true of Halifax in part, we make an error if we take the whole passage to be a portrait of him.   Pope took a delight in drawing satirical characters that are not wholly true of anyone. When the cap fits, anyone is at liberty to put it on; but Pope's commentators have found much occupation in trying to fit his caps to particular heads, and they blame Pope—they sometimes even accuse him of dishonesty—when the cap does not fit at all parts.

That the character of Atticus was wholly suggested by Addison is certain; but do not let us forget that, in its final form, it is a portrait of

Atticus, and do not let us miss the significance of the alteration.

When Pope began to make his name, Addison was already a man of established reputation, and he was kind to the young poet, who was proud to be encouraged. But as the young poet became more conscious of his powers he began to detect an air of patronage, and to realize that the encouragement he received was more discreet than enthusiastic. There was no enthusiasm in Addison's nature,—he was controlled and reserved; in private life he showed the restraint and the balance and the correctness which make the distinctive character of his essays in *The Spectator* and give them a place by themselves in English literature. Gradually the difference of sixteen years in their ages made their personal relations difficult to adjust when the younger man, who was abnormally sensitive, and very ambitious, had attained to fame, and when the older man found that his encouragement was no longer required. Then something happened that Pope did not like. He may have put the wrong construction on it; but he felt so strongly that he was moved to tell Addison what he thought, and this he did in a character-sketch in verse. Years afterwards, when Addison was dead, Pope inserted this sketch in his *Epistle to Arbuthnot,*—a receptacle for more than one piece that he was unwilling to lose,—but he took out some particular allusions; he took out everything that necessarily associated it with Addison, and, to show that he was then thinking of the type and not the individual, he altered the name to Atticus. It is a mistake to speak, as a critic has recently done, of the inserted praise. Admiration of Addison's great qualities is at the very basis of his satire,—admiration that has been thwarted and for the time has gone sour. Pope felt that he had been injured, and the sense of injury moved him to describe how great talents could be marred by petty personal weaknesses.

> Peace to all such! but were there One whose fires
> True Genius kindles, and fair Fame inspires,
> Blest with each Talent and each Art to please,
> And born to write, converse, and live with ease:
> Shou'd such a man, too fond to rule alone,
> Bear, like the *Turk*, no brother near the throne,
> View him with scornful, yet with jealous eyes,
> And hate for Arts that caus'd himself to rise;
> Damn with faint praise, assent with civil leer,
> And without sneering, teach the rest to sneer;
> Willing to wound, and yet afraid to strike,
> Just hint a fault, and hesitate dislike;
> Alike reserv'd to blame, or to commend,
> A tim'rous foe, and a suspicious friend,
> Dreading ev'n fools, by Flatterers besieg'd,
> And so obliging that he ne'er oblig'd;
> Like *Cato*, give his little Senate laws,
> And sit attentive to his own applause;
> While Wits and Templers ev'ry sentence raise,

And wonder with a foolish face of praise.
Who but must laugh, if such a man there be?
Who would not weep, if *Atticus* were he!

Every word tells, and every word is an easy and significant word.   The whole passage is a crescendo of controlled resentment till the sudden drop at the conclusion, which turns to ridicule the petty faults that are unworthy of a great man.

In contrast to this intense passage let me quote Pope's light-hearted rejoinder to the question which I suppose we have all heard,—what is the use of poetry and poets? It has the incidental interest of containing his ultimate verdict on Addison as a writer, and never has Addison received higher praise:

Of little use the Man you may suppose,
Who says in verse what others say in prose;
Yet let me show, a Poet's of some weight,
And (tho' no Soldier) useful to the State.
What will a Child learn sooner than a song?
What better teach a Foreigner the tongue?
What's long or short, each accent where to place,
And speak in publick with some sort of grace?
I scarce can think him such a worthless thing,
Unless he praise some monster of a King,
Or Virtue, or Religion turn to sport,
To please a lewd, or unbelieving Court.
Unhappy Dryden!—In all Charles's days,
Roscommon only boasts unspotted Bays;
And in our own (excuse some Courtly stains)
No whiter page than Addison remains.

He, from the taste obscene reclaims our Youth,
And sets the Passions on the side of Truth;
Forms the soft bosom with the gentlest art,
And pours each human Virtue in the heart.
Let Ireland tell, how Wit upheld her cause,
Her Trade supported, and supply'd her Laws;
And leave on SWIFT this grateful verse ingrav'd,
The Rights a court attack'd, a Poet sav'd.
Behold the hand that wrought a Nation's cure,
Stretch'd to relieve the Idiot and the Poor,
Proud Vice to brand, or injur'd Worth adorn,
And stretch the Ray to Ages yet unborn.
Not but there are, who merit other palms;
Hopkins and Sternhold glad the heart with Psalms:
The Boys and Girls whom Charity maintains,
Implore your help in these pathetic strains:
How could Devotion touch the country pews,
Unless the Gods bestow'd a proper Muse?
Verse chears their leisure, Verse assists their work,
Verse prays for Peace, or sings down Pope and Turk.
The silenc'd Preacher yields to potent strain,
And feels that grace his pray'r besought in vain;
The blessing thrills thro' all the lab'ring throng,
And Heav'n is won by violence of Song.

You will have noticed how this passage changes in mood. It begins familiarly, almost frivolously; presently it becomes serious in its glowing tribute to the white page of Addison and the benefits that Swift conferred on Ireland; and then it reverts to the lighter manner when it pictures the boys and girls in charity schools singing the metrical version of the Psalms at the top of their voices, and the congregations that hope to win heaven by violence of song. And as the mood changes the verse changes; now it moves slowly and now it trips along.

These two passages illustrate the range of Pope's satire from severity to gentle twitting. To most people he is best known as a satirist, to many only as a satirist. But those who know him well are not all disposed to give his satires the first place. This very sensitive man could feel, as is the way with such men, the warmth of affection as truly as the bitterness of resentment, and I believe that if we take the trouble to know him in both moods we prefer him in the gentler, when he speaks—to use his own words—the language of the heart. I confess that I get tired of his bitterness, as I get tired of the bitterness of everyone. I do not think that he shows to best advantage—and I know no one who does—when he is smarting under the sense of personal injury or fancying an affront. I must admire his mastery of his weapons, and his courage in attack; unlike his traducers, he never attacked the dead; but I like him better when he is not disturbed by "the strong antipathy of good to bad". You will remember that Charles Lamb chose Pope as a person he would wish to have seen, and that the choice puzzled his hearers as it has puzzled many since, who think of Pope first and last as a satirist. But he was equally a master of the friendly epistle, and there we find the compliments which Hazlitt termed "divine", and which Lamb called "the finest that were ever paid by the wit of man".

Take the epistle to Robert Harley, Earl of Oxford, chief minister to Queen Anne during the last years of her reign.   When his political enemies came into office on the accession of George I, they moved for his impeachment, and he was confined to the Tower for more than a year awaiting trial. The proceedings were abandoned, but Oxford retired from politics to live out his life in peace amid his great library.   After recalling the days when Oxford would quit

> the Farce of State,
> The sober follies of the Wise and Great,

and escape to the company of the wits of the Scriblerus Club, Pope addresses him thus:

> And sure if ought below the Seats Divine
> Can touch Immortals, 'tis a Soul like thine:
> A Soul supreme, in each hard Instance try'd,
> Above all Pain, all Passion, and all Pride,
> The Rage of Pow'r, the Blast of publick Breath,
> The Lust of Lucre, and the Dread of Death.
> In vain to Desarts thy Retreat is made;
> The Muse attends thee to the silent Shade:
> 'Tis hers, the brave Man's latest Steps to trace,
> Re-judge his Acts, and dignify Disgrace.
> When Int'rest calls off all her sneaking Train,
> When all th' Oblig'd desert, and all the Vain;
> She waits, or to the Scaffold, or the Cell,

When the last ling'ring Friend has bid farewel.
Ev'n now she shades thy Evening Walk with Bays,
(No Hireling she, no Prostitute to Praise)
Ev'n now, observant of the parting Ray,
Eyes the calm Sun-set of thy Various Day,
Thro' Fortune's Cloud One truly Great can see,
Nor fears to tell, that MORTIMER is He.

Satire or compliment, every line is fully charged.
Pope tried to pack into each couplet as much as it
would hold. He found that verse was distinct from
prose in requiring brevity of expression, even in
enabling him to use the fewest words that were
needed. As a prose writer he is not markedly con-
cise; I do not think that he is so concise as Swift.
But it was not an idle compliment that Swift paid
him when he said:

> In Pope I cannot read a line,
> But with a sigh I wish it mine;
> When he can in one couplet fix
> More sense than I can do in six.

There are some poets whom we can enjoy without
bending our minds to what they say. We are
carried on by the music of their verse. The
reader of *The Faerie Queene* is sometimes advised
to begin by subjecting himself to the sheer beauty
of the sound. Many passages in Shelley win us at
once by their magic, but give us trouble when we
come to examine the development of the thought
or the significance of the phrasing. The glamour

that Pope casts upon us—those of us who are fortunate enough to feel the glamour—is of a different kind. The music of his verse contributes to it; but it also comes from the precision of his ideas and the rapidity of their ordered succession.

"What is a new thought?" The question was asked by Boileau, and he gave his answer. "It is not", he said, "a thought which nobody has had, and perhaps nobody ought to have had, but it is a thought which everyone might have had and someone has been the first to express"—something that we all recognize at once to be true, and then could wish that we had said ourselves. Therein lies a source of the pleasure which we derive from the poetry of the eighteenth century. To what we might have thought, or perhaps were vaguely thinking, we again and again find that Pope has given convincing expression; and these words are only a dull echo of his own words:

> Something, whose truth convinced at sight we find,
> That gives us back the image of our mind.

So far I have said little about Pope's versification. I hope to deal with that to-morrow, and with another master of the heroic couplet, Samuel Johnson.

II

The Heroic Couplet—Johnson

IN dealing with the poetic diction of the eighteenth century I had occasion to quote Coleridge's saying that its main source was Pope's translation of the *Iliad*. Let me now quote another portion of the same sentence,—"the almost faultless position and choice of words in Mr. Pope's *original* compositions, particularly in his Satires and moral Essays". It will serve as the starting point for what has now to be said about his versification.

"Almost faultless choice of words" and "almost faultless position of words". The most obvious meaning of this high praise can be tested by our own experience. Whenever we repeat one of Pope's couplets without being quite word perfect, we invariably find that the words which have eluded us are better than any we may have supplied in their place; and if we examine the alterations which Pope himself made we also invariably find that they are improvements. A comparison of Pope's variants is a lesson in style. I am not thinking of his *Dunciad*, where the revision extends to structure and subject-matter, but of his shorter uncontroversial poems, which afford as good illustrations as we could wish of his sense of the *mot juste*. One of the outstanding lines in his address to the Earl of Oxford which I quoted yesterday must have struck you as being

Above all Pain, all Passion, and all Pride.

It was a line which struck Hazlitt; but we may doubt if it would have struck him had it remained in its original form,—

Above all Pain, all Anger, and all Pride.

This change is characteristic of Pope's changes in general. He aims at enriching the meaning and the music of his lines,—and the meaning and the music aid each other. We shall not easily find a poet who illustrates the unrelenting pursuit of this ideal more consistently.

But what Coleridge says about the almost faultless position and choice of words has a wider significance. It means that Pope was not dominated by his poetical measure, that, unlike many of his imitators, he was not the victim of the heroic couplet. He does with it what he likes. He chooses the proper words, and they go into their proper places.

I said yesterday that the heroic couplet has a way of limiting or controlling the poet who is not fully its master. Let us look at it to-day from the point of view of the reader. It is not the easiest of English measures to recite. When the sense is completed by two lines at a time, or when two lines form a separable clause, the reader always runs some risk of making the measure too prominent. If he makes it too prominent he will make it monotonous. To use the words of Keats, he will sway about upon a rocking-horse. But he will not make the verse of Pope monotonous if he thinks about what he is reading. Pope must always be read with more attention to his meaning than to his measure. This may seem a platitude. But does everyone escape from sing-song when he recites heroic couplets? Attend to Pope's meaning and his measure will look after itself. The sense controls the movement. As the sense passes from grave to gay, from lively to severe, the verse moves with it, the music changes. The heroic couplet, that very difficult instrument, is capable of producing an astonishing range of effects, and different masters make it produce different music.

When we go to the *Comédie Française* in Paris and hear the actors who have been trained in the tradition declaiming the lines of Corneille and Racine, we do not complain of monotony. But we are hearing couplets, and couplets as strongly marked as those of Pope.

If you will allow the rhythm to be given by the sense, you will find that Pope's line, which is technically of five feet, has not the invariable number of five clearly marked accents. I do not mean to suggest that every reader ought to read Pope in the same way, or even that the same

reader will always read him in the same way. No
two executants give us the same rendering of a
piece of music, and much the same is true of the
readers of poetry. Different readers may take the
same line slightly differently,—in other words there
may be some slight variation in the degree and the
placing of emphasis and in the pace,—but the sense
will compel them to agree that in a very large
number of Pope's lines there are four strong
accents, and in others more than five.

Let me illustrate from passages that I have not
already quoted:

> How happy is the blameless Vestal's lot!
> The world forgetting, by the world forgot.
> Eternal sunshine of the spotless mind!
> Each pray'r accepted, and each wish resign'd;
> Labour and rest, that equal periods keep;
> "Obedient slumbers that can wake and weep".

Only one of these six lines has unquestionably five
strong accents, and you will agree that if we are to
bring out the full force of "Each pray'r accepted,
and each wish resign'd", we must lay emphasis on
the recurring "each",—which will make it a line
of six accents. Or take this passage of another
kind:

> Behold the child, by Nature's kindly law,
> Pleas'd with a rattle, tickled with a straw:
> Some livelier play-thing gives his youth delight,
> A little louder, but as empty quite:

> Scarfs, garters, gold, amuse his riper stage,
> And beads and pray'r-books are the toys of age:
> Pleas'd with *this* bauble still, as *that* before,
> 'Till tir'd he sleeps, and Life's poor play is o'er.

It is Pope's habit to vary the line of five accents with the line of four (in some passages the line of four predominates) and in these two passages that have just been quoted he introduces lines of six. Sometimes there are only three, as in the second line of this couplet—

> Safe in the hand of one disposing Pow'r,
> Or in the natal, or the mortal Hour.

And sometimes there are more than six. How are we to read these lines?—

> Oh, be thou blest with all that Heav'n can send!
> Long Health, long Youth, long Pleasure, and a Friend.

We must give full force to "long" each time it occurs; and we must accentuate "Health", "Youth", "Pleasure", and "Friend". As I read it, the second line has seven clearly marked words.

Again, and as a consequence, the pace varies. Some lines carry us along rapidly, but others will be read slowly if we render their full meaning:

> But grant, in Public, Men sometimes are shown,
> A Woman's seen in Private life alone.

Take the first line rapidly and we lose much of what Pope is saying. It is a good instance of

Pope's habit of packing as much into a line as it will contain.

All this I suggest that we should bear in mind when next we are told that the heroic couplets of Pope are monotonous.

No one habitually gives the heroic couplet a more rapid movement than Dryden.   As Johnson said, we read "in a hurry of delight".   By contrast Johnson's own verses move slowly; nowhere shall we find any that are more weighty and massive. Johnson refuses to be read quickly.   He and Goldsmith are the two great masters of the heroic couplet after Pope,—I am inclined to say its only masters.   It is the measure in which they express themselves most easily and most fully.

Read any of the great passages in *The Vanity of Human Wishes* and we shall at once admit that it could not have been written by Dryden, or Pope, or Goldsmith.   Let us also admit that Johnson is not a poet of wide range.   He has not left many verses, and they have one prevailing quality or manner.   Indeed we may say that his reputation as a poet must rest on one poem, *The Vanity of Human Wishes*.   But it stands by itself in English literature.   Nowhere else in all our poetry is the theme that "all is Vanity" given so majestic expression.

The poem is a modern rendering from classical literature, an adaptation of the same kind as Pope's

Satires and Epistles. Pope had chosen Horace, and Johnson chose Juvenal, with whom he felt some kinship. "The peculiarity of Juvenal", he was to say some thirty years later, "is a mixture of gaiety and stateliness, of pointed sentences and declamatory grandeur." This may pass as a description of his own peculiarity. His gaiety was of the kind that wells up from deep feeling, and there was little occasion for the display of it in this poem, but stateliness and pointed sentences and declamatory grandeur were his birthright. About the theme of Juvenal's tenth satire he could learn nothing from Juvenal that he had not already learned from his own experience. What he takes from Juvenal is the framework, the rough plan. When he is obviously following Juvenal he is, as we should expect, not at his best. Some difficult and even awkward lines invite us to consult the original. Within the framework he speaks for himself.

The cumbrous first lines have met with much amused comment,—

> Let Observation with extensive view
> Survey mankind, from China to Peru.

Coleridge was not the first to point out that they only said "let observation with extensive observation observe mankind extensively", nor was he the last. Johnson's rendering of Juvenal's open-

ing cannot compare with the brilliant rendering
of Dryden:

> Look round the habitable world, how few
> Know their own good; or, knowing it, pursue.
> How void of reason are our hopes and fears!
> What in the conduct of our life appears
> So well design'd, so luckily begun,
> But, when we have our wish, we wish undone?

Of Dryden's translation of Juvenal as a whole
Johnson remarked that it is possible to improve
upon it, "some passages excepted, which will never
be excelled", and it is permissible to believe that
one of the passages which he had in mind was the
opening in which he himself had failed.   But as a
rule Johnson is not a very good starter.   Of many
of his *Rambler* essays we could omit the first
paragraph without notable loss.   The engine is
rather slow in heating up, and of *The Vanity of
Human Wishes* we shall probably all say that it
does not begin to move easily and with full power
till, in its first original passage, it illustrates the
vanity of worldly grandeur in the person of Wolsey.
The search for power does not bring happiness.
Nor does the calm pursuit of learning have its
certain rewards:

> There mark what Ills the Scholar's Life assail,
> Toil, Envy, Want, the Patron, and the Jail.

Military prowess brought Charles XII to disaster.
No part of the poem is better known than this

picture of the dauntless soldier—"a Frame of
Adamant, a Soul of Fire", the terror of Europe,
whose

> . . . Fall was destin'd to a barren Strand,
> A petty Fortress, and a dubious Hand.

Beauty has its perils, even virtue has its crosses.
Yet the poem is not depressing. Somehow it
reconciles us to the human lot, and largely for this
reason, that it faces the facts unflinchingly and is
written with the wisdom of acceptance.

The poem raises questions which we are bound
to face. We may ask, to begin with, whether
Johnson has not given greater expression to the
same theme in prose. What of *Rasselas*, the prose
Vanity of Human Wishes? Is not this novel, if so
it may be called, a fuller and richer exposition of
the futility of the search for happiness? "Ye who
listen with credulity to the whispers of fancy, and
pursue with eagerness the phantoms of hope; who
expect that age will perform the promises of youth,
and that the deficiencies of the present day will be
supplied by the morrow; attend to the history of
Rasselas Prince of Abissinia." Rasselas is brought
up in a happy valley, in the midst of all that art
and nature can bestow, but he is unsatisfied.
"Man", he says, "surely has some latent sense for
which this place affords no gratification." So he
leaves the valley in the hope of gratifying this
sense, and sees all kinds of men, all searching for

happiness; and in the end he resolves that he may
as well return to Abyssinia. In this prose tale
there is a greater wealth of thought, which is
communicated to us more intimately than in the
poem, and with an element of irony that the poem
does not allow. It admits us more freely to the
workings of Johnson's mind. And yet I think
that those of us with whom *Rasselas* is a favourite
book, and who even hold that admiration of it is
an essential in the proper appreciation of Johnson,
will yet admit that the poem moves us more deeply
in its greater passages, and has a command of
pathos which the tale does not reveal.

This raises another question. Was verse John-
son's natural mode of expression? We may admit
at once that his proper language was prose. His
thoughts did not naturally run to verse. When
they did voluntary move harmonious numbers,
they were the numbers of prose. There he differed
from Pope, who could express himself in verse
more easily and convincingly. Read Pope's prose
and we shall find that in comparison with his verse
it is—to use Milton's phrase—his "left hand".
And take Dryden. He is remarkable in being
equally a master of both. Read his essays and
you are convinced that prose was his true medium;
read his verse and you have no doubt that his
thoughts naturally turned to verse. Dryden him-
self admits as much in his last Preface: "thoughts,

such as they are, come crowding in so fast upon me, that my only difficulty is to choose or to reject, to run them into verse, or to give them the other harmony of prose." But Johnson has no divided allegiance; he is normally a prose man. All this we may admit without questioning that *The Vanity of Human Wishes* is a great poem. The successive character-sketches are in their own style master-pieces. No one will suggest how they could have been done better. Each is complete in itself and can be taken out of its setting, but their place in the framework sets them off to full advantage. The effect of the poem is cumulative; we are gripped more strongly the further we proceed. The impression is never broken or injured. The poem has perfect harmony of mood.

Johnson's method of composition conduced to this harmony. "When composing", he said to Boswell, "I have generally had them [*i.e.*, *his verses*] in my mind, perhaps fifty at a time, walking up and down in my room; and then I have written them down, and often, from laziness, have written only half lines. I have written a hundred lines in a day. I remember I wrote a hundred lines of *The Vanity of Human Wishes* in a day." He has described three different methods of composition in his *Life of Pope*, and must have had himself in mind when describing the first of them: "Some employ at once memory and invention, and, with

little intermediate use of the pen, form and polish
large masses by continued meditation, and write
their productions only when, in their own opinion,
they have completed them. It is related of Virgil
that his custom was to pour out a great number of
verses in the morning, and pass the day in re-
trenching exuberances and correcting inaccuracies.
The method of Pope . . . was to write his first
thoughts in his first words, and gradually to
amplify, decorate, rectify, and refine them." The
first of these methods, which is Johnson's method,
makes for sequence and harmony of thought; and
in Johnson's great passages we are carried on with-
out interruption, though we are aware that every
word is telling, that every word has been considered
and approved. On the other hand, and in illustra-
tion of what Johnson says about Pope's method,
we can easily point to passages in Pope's poems
which evidently came to him in couplets and tend
to break up into couplets,— passages where we miss
the continuity and the larger movement as of a
wave to be found in his best work. In *The Vanity
of Human Wishes*, despite all the care that has
been taken with the details, we lack the sense of the
wave when Johnson is remembering Juvenal and
attending to the framework.

Now you may say—and this raises another
question—that his verse is the product of a severely
intellectual process. Certainly the reader of *The*

Vanity of Human Wishes is always aware of the powerful mind that controlled and shaped it. Johnson would not have said, as Wordsworth said in *The Waggoner*:

> Nor is it I who play the part,
> But a shy spirit in my heart
> That comes and goes.

The shy spirit in Johnson's heart was taken in charge by his intellect, its promptings were submitted to scrutiny and regulated. But speak as we like of the intellectual quality of *The Vanity of Human Wishes*, we have all the same experience, if we read the poem aright, that what remains most vividly in our memories is its emotional content.

It is emotion of a type which I am tempted to call depersonalized. Johnson never speaks in his own person; the one passage in which we can clearly detect him thinking of himself is his description of the life of the scholar. We are familiar with the other kind of poem in which the author is the centre of his world. He proceeds from himself outwards, and the reader accepts as widely true what the poet began by saying of himself. This kind of emotional poem is at once recognized for what it is. But who is at the centre of *The Vanity of Human Wishes?* Is it Johnson? Is any one person there more than another? We know that the poem must be written by a man of deep feeling and strong intellect, but what would be the effect if, after having directed our minds to our common lot, the author should begin to speak about himself?

It is a matter of method. Wordsworth begins with himself and takes us along with him, and we know that he will take us far beyond himself. He sees a small flower buffeted by rain and storm; he describes it, and we see it; we wait for the moral reflection; and it comes at the conclusion of the poem:

> To be a Prodigal's Favourite,—then, worse truth,
> A Miser's Pensioner,—behold our lot!
> O Man, that from thy fair and shining youth
> Age might but take the things Youth needed not.

He revisits a scene which he remembered with gratitude and affection:

> Five years have past; five summers, with the length
> Of five long winters! and again I hear
> These waters, rolling from their mountain-springs
> With a soft inland murmur.

Thus Wordsworth begins the greatest of his poems on what Nature meant to him.

Johnson's method is, so to speak, to begin at the other end. He begins with the big world, from China to Peru, he generalizes, and then he works down to the particular illustration, but not to himself, though the truth of what he says is recognized by every one of us individually. He finds his illustrations in well-known historical characters, as in Wolsey, or Charles XII; or he draws the picture of a type, such as the earnest unselfish, unhappy scholar; or he paints the misfortunes that do not pass by even virtuous old age.

This last passage I will now quote. It is not the best known passage in the poem; but I do not know who else could have written it; and I quote it for this further reason that it reveals Johnson in a light in which he is not generally regarded, as a master of pathos.

But grant, the Virtues of a temp'rate Prime
Bless with an Age exempt from Scorn or Crime;
An Age that melts in unperceiv'd Decay,
And glides in modest Innocence away;
Whose peaceful Day Benevolence endears,
Whose Night congratulating Conscience cheers;
The gen'ral Fav'rite as the gen'ral Friend:
Such Age there is, and who could wish its End?
 Yet ev'n on this her Load Misfortune flings,
To press the weary Minutes flagging Wings:
New Sorrow rises as the Day returns,
A Sister sickens, or a Daughter mourns.
Now Kindred Merit fills the sable Bier,
Now lacerated Friendship claims a Tear.
Year chases Year, Decay pursues Decay,
Still drops some Joy from with'ring Life away;
New Forms arise, and diff'rent Views engage,
Superfluous lags the Vet'ran on the Stage,
Till pitying Nature signs the last Release,
And bids afflicted Worth retire to Peace.
 But few there are whom Hours like these await,
Who set unclouded in the Gulphs of Fate.
From *Lydia*'s Monarch should the Search descend,

By *Solon* caution'd to regard his End,
In Life's last Scene what Prodigies surprise,
Fears of the Brave, and Follies of the Wise?
From *Marlb'rough*'s Eyes the Streams of Dotage flow,
And *Swift* expires a Driv'ler and a Show.

"The deep and pathetic morality" of this poem, said Sir Walter Scott, "has often extracted tears from those whose eyes wander dry over pages professedly sentimental." He must have been thinking in particular of this passage. One of its lines, "Superfluous lags the Vet'ran on the Stage", he came to apply to himself. He speaks of the "sublime strain of morality" with which the poem closes. The Wizard of the North who had enchanted his generation went back for security to *The Vanity of Human Wishes*. "He had often said to me", a friend records, "that neither his own nor any modern popular style of composition was that from which he derived most pleasure. I asked him what it was. He answered—Johnson's; and that he had more pleasure in reading *London* and *The Vanity of Human Wishes*, than any other poetical composition he could mention; and I think I never saw his countenance more indicative of high admiration than while reciting aloud from those productions."

In every line of this highly emotional passage we feel the strong intellectual grip. We never doubt that the poet is in perfect control; but verse like this is not the product of a severely rational process. Much that has been written about the poetry of the eighteenth century seems to me to be vitiated by the fallacy that reason and emotion are necessarily at strife.

The passage which I have read also raises the question of the place of abstract terms in poetry. I do not think that we have been disturbed by them; on the contrary, they may seem to some of us to make the beauty of such lines as these:

> An Age that melts in unperceiv'd Decay,
> And glides in modest Innocence away;
> Whose peaceful Day Benevolence endears,
> Whose Night congratulating Conscience cheers.

Abstract terms are the direct consequence of a method which does not pass from the particular to the general, but is concerned primarily with a general truth and may or may not find for it the particular illustration. The poet who is intent on remarking general properties and large appearances, to use Imlac's words in *Rasselas*, will require sooner or later words of general meaning. Once again we have to say that every instance must be treated on its merits. There is no greater master of the abstract word than Shakespeare. The only question that we have to ask ourselves is,—does the abstract word suit the occasion? I cannot hesitate to answer that it does in the lines which I have quoted, and that without it Johnson could not have conveyed the impression which he intended. But I am not therefore prepared to praise his poem on the Ant, where the phraseology does not seem to me quite to carry its weight.[1]

And I think that we must all be struck with the deep sonorous music of these lines, and recognize the part which it plays in the total impression. We are frequently told that Johnson had a bad ear. That is the compendious method of dismissing such remarks of his on metre as we do not like. But I submit on the evidence of these lines that he had a very good ear; and further evidence is to be found in his revision of the poem. In the first edition he had written—

And Sloth's bland Opiates shed their Fumes in vain.

He gets rid of "bland", an epithet which contributed little to the meaning; but he is more concerned to reduce the number of the sibilants. In its final form it is soporific—

And Sloth effuse her opiate fumes in vain.

Remembering what he said about "representative metre", I will not suggest that he was here betrayed into making the sound seem an echo to the sense. We may be content to acknowledge his

---

[1] To Wordsworth the Ant was "a babble of words". But he did not deny himself the aid of abstract terms. In his *Letter to a Friend of Robert Burns*, when commenting on Tam o' Shanter's behaviour in the inn, he says that "conjugal fidelity archly bends to the service of general benevolence".

care for the sound in an alteration which left the sense unaffected.

Johnson's ear was very sensitive to what he calls "collisions of consonants" and in particular to the sibilant. In his judicial estimate of his friend Collins, he says that "his diction was often harsh, unskilfully laboured, and injudiciously selected. . . . His lines commonly are of slow motion, clogged and impeded with clusters of consonants." Johnson was thinking of such a line as

> The Year's best Sweets shall duteous rise,

a line which, with a sibilant in every word, Tennyson was to select for condemnation. But Gray had already said in a private letter, written immediately on the appearance of the volume which contained the *Ode to Evening*, that Collins had a bad ear. No one has ever doubted Gray's right to offer his opinion on word-music; whatever criticisms are made on his poetry, none is directed against the sound of his lines. Nor has anyone doubted Tennyson's right to speak on that matter. Gray and Tennyson agree about Collins's ear, and Johnson agrees with them.

How, then, has it been suggested that Johnson was deaf to the music of verse? The suggestion is made by those who maintain that Johnson's interest in verse was severely intellectual, and they find support for it in his declared preference of the heroic couplet over blank verse, and in his be-littling of *Lycidas*.

Of *Lycidas* he says that "the diction is harsh, the rhymes uncertain, and the numbers unpleas-ing". Again he uses the word "harsh", and it was a word which he used frequently. The songs in *Comus* he describes as "harsh in their diction"; the language of Gray's *Pindaric Odes* is said to be "laboured into harshness". In all the large body of criticism which he himself sent to the press there is little which we cannot easily understand, whether or not we agree; but why *Lycidas* of all Milton's poems should be said to exhibit harshness remains a difficulty. I cannot think that the word "harsh" is normally used by a man whose ear is insensitive.

We may not have paid enough attention to the words with which his studied depreciation of *Lycidas* begins,—"one of the poems on which much praise has been bestowed is *Lycidas*". He means "too much praise". Had no one praised *Lycidas* we may be certain that he would have written differently. His manner suggests that he is fight-ing a received opinion. He had begun to fight it in *The Rambler* (No. 37), and the time had come to be done with it. The early work of Milton was distracting attention from *Paradise Lost*, by the side of which *Lycidas* was but a trifle. "All the

minor poems he dispatched without much anxiety"
before proceeding to the examination of the great
epic which he calls one of the greatest productions
of the human mind.

Johnson had already examined the versification
of *Paradise Lost* in three of his essays in *The
Rambler* (Nos. 86, 88, 90), and they form a little
treatise which should not be ignored when his
comments on the versification of any other poem
are in question.

"It is pronounced by Dryden", we read, "that
a line of monosyllables is almost always harsh."
I have not discovered, on a hasty search, that
Dryden used the word "harsh", but Dryden
certainly does say that " 'tis all we can do to give
sufficient sweetness to our language", and John-
son's argument in these three papers is largely a
development of what Dryden had said in the
Preface to his *Aeneid* and intended to develop in
his unwritten treatise on Prosody. The trouble
about our monosyllables, according to Johnson, is
that, "being of Teutonic original or formed by
contraction", they "commonly begin and end with
consonants"; and the trouble seemed to him to
extend to longer words. The difference of har-
mony arising principally from the collocation of
vowels and consonants, he illustrates from two
neighbouring lines in *Paradise Lost*.

Rolls o'er Elysian flow'rs her amber stream

he contrasts with

Bind their resplendent locks inwreath'd with beams.

He regrets Milton's elisions, again for the same
reason that our language is already overstocked
with consonants; he even questions if elisions are
not unsuitable to the genius of the English
tongue.   Always comparing English with Latin,
Greek, or Italian, he wonders whether we have not
injured our language, for purposes of poetry, by
dropping our inflexions; and in particular he shows
unexpected interest in the Chaucerian final *e*
which Tyrwhitt was soon to take under his
protection: "There is reason to believe that we
have negligently lost part of our vowels, and that
the silent *e* which our ancestors added to most of
our monosyllables was once vocal. By this de-
truncation of our syllables our language is over-
stocked with consonants, and it is more necessary
to add vowels to the beginning of words than to
cut them off from the end" [No. 88]. Milton
seemed to Johnson to be "fully convinced of the
unfitness of our language for smooth versification",
and to deserve the highest praise for what he
accomplished. "If the poetry of Milton be ex-
amined", he says, "with regard to the pauses and
flow of his verses into each other, it will appear
that he has performed all that our language would
admit." His conclusion is that Milton's "skill in

harmony was not less than his invention or his learning".

All this about *Paradise Lost*.   And with all this in mind we must approach with circumspection what he says about *Lycidas*.   A clue to what he meant by saying that "the diction is harsh" should be sought for in these early essays.

Johnson explains why he prefers the heroic couplet to blank verse, but he is careful to tell us that he cannot wish *Paradise Lost* to be other than it is,—"I cannot prevail on myself to wish that Milton had been a rhymer."   He says that "Poetry may subsist without rhyme, but English poetry will not often please; nor can rhyme ever be safely spared but where the subject is able to support itself."   He thought that blank verse was rightly used in Thomson's *Seasons* and Young's *Night Thoughts*; in these, as in *Paradise Lost*, the subjects were of self-supporting magnitude.   But by the middle of the century blank verse had become the customary measure for the didactic or philosophic or meditative poem, and in this new fashion English poetry seemed to him to be depriving itself of a means of giving pleasure.   Of all the poems written in blank verse between Young's *Night Thoughts* and Cowper's *Task* how many are we glad to remember?   Akenside's *Pleasures of the Imagination*—in part, and Dyer's *Fleece*—in part, and possibly one or two others; but during the last thirty years of Johnson's life (*The Task* appeared about the time of his death) the memorable poem in blank verse does not become more common.   Again I suspect that, while his admiration of *Paradise Lost* remained undiminished, his doubts about blank verse were strengthened by the blank verse of his contemporaries.

But it is time to return to Johnson's own poetry, and so to close.   I have endeavoured to deal with some of his critical statements by which I believe his own critics have allowed themselves to be misled, for I cannot think that had they confined their attention to his verse they would have questioned his sense of the music of poetry.   If I seem to you to have spoken about him at disproportionate length, I would urge that many of the questions which he raises are relevant to eighteenth century poetry as a whole.   It is a poetry which is concerned in the main with man in his ordinary experiences.   It is not given to looking before and after and pining for what is not.   Perhaps it is a little too grown-up for that.   If you wish to find the enthusiasms and exaltations or the depressions of youth, you had better go elsewhere. It prefers to deal with what man is, and knows, and feels.   And that is why so much of this poetry retains a secure hold on the affections of the English-speaking peoples.   Gray in his *Elegy Written in a Country Church Yard* or Goldsmith in his *Deserted*

Village tells us only what we all know or feel, and better than we could express it ourselves. These poems "abound with images which find a mirror in every mind and with sentiments to which every bosom returns an echo". The best poetry of the eighteenth century gives us the security which comes from looking at things as they are. It is rich in moral wisdom and in emotion expressed in memorable verse.

III

Thomson—Burns

MAY I remind you that I am not endeavouring to offer you a new estimate of the poetry of the eighteenth century? It is true that, to use Johnson's words, I have remarked some of its general properties and large appearances, but I am less directly concerned with these than with the merits of representative authors and even of particular passages. As I warned you at the outset, I have in mind such matters as seem to me to deserve fuller consideration than they have yet received. I ask you to distrust the familiar labels,—"classical", "neo-classical", "pseudo-classical", "pre-romantic", and all the others. I sometimes doubt if we shall ever understand the poetry of this century till we get rid of the terms "classical" and "romantic" in one and all of their forms. Johnson, Coleridge, and Hazlitt—perhaps our three greatest critics—did not find the need of them; nor should we.

Everyone of us who is concerned with the teaching of English literature is aware that whereas there is general agreement about Elizabethan poetry and the poetry of the seventeenth century, there are at least two "schools of thought" about the poetry of the eighteenth. To one school the century is mainly of interest as being the seed-time of the poetry which blossomed in the days of Wordsworth and Coleridge. Even those who do not profess adherence to this school can remember the occasions when as the spirits failed and the eyes grew dim and two or three questions had yet to be set before the examination paper was complete, the temptation to jot down something about the first signs of the "Romantic Revival" proved irresistible. All of us, at least the older of us, have at some stage been taught to picture the marches and the counter-marches which, about the middle of the century, began to disturb the Peace of the Augustans, and the final triumphal onslaught of *Lyrical Ballads*. The good verse, we were asked to believe, belonged to the future, and the poor verse or the indifferent verse was in its proper place. Good poets, like Gray, were said to be born out of their time. Somehow Nature had made a slip and dropped a poet in an age of prose.

Others prefer the modest alternative that when a poet seems to have got into the wrong place what is wrong is our idea of the place. Like every other century the eighteenth was an age of transition, but we need not therefore assume that its poets were engaged in one long campaign. The good poets of the eighteenth century spoke frankly about each other, as poets usually do; and though their aims might be divergent, they were always as ready as poets have ever been to acknowledge merit when they found it.

So far I have chosen to speak mainly of Pope and Johnson. I now turn to two other representative poets of the century,—James Thomson and Robert Burns.

Both of them were Scots, and neither could have written as he did had he not been a Scot. Each has been hailed, rightly or wrongly, as introducing a new element into our poetry. The work of every good poet must be in some sense novel. No man, as Johnson said, was ever great by imitation; and whether or not this is invariably true, it is certainly true of the artist. But neither Thomson nor Burns ever imagined himself to be a rebel.

Nor must we imagine that Pope, or Johnson, believed the empire of Wit to be limited and defined. They may have charted the portions of it with which they were familiar, but they knew that it was always expanding. Pope had maintained in the *Essay on Criticism* that anything is permissible provided it succeeds, but that the poet was less likely to succeed if he neglected what could be learned from his great predecessors. Should

> Some lucky licence answer to the full
> The intent proposed, that licence is a rule.

Thomson's *Winter* was a new kind of poem, but it fulfilled its purpose, and Pope welcomed it. He

came to know Thomson and in the next edition of
Winter Thomson inserted a glowing tribute to his
friendship:

> Or from the muses' hill will *Pope* descend,
> To raise the sacred hour, to make it smile,
> And with the social spirit warm the heart:
> For tho' not sweeter his own *Homer* sings,
> Yet is his life the more endearing song.

Similarly Pope urged the publication of Akenside's
Pleasures of the Imagination, a poem so novel that
the publisher to whom it was submitted did not
know what to make of it.   "I have heard Dodsley,
by whom it was published, relate", says Johnson,
"that when the copy was offered him the price
demanded for it, which was an hundred and twenty
pounds, being such as he was not inclined to give
precipitately, he carried the work to Pope, who,
having looked into it, advised him not to make a
niggardly offer; for 'this was no every-day writer'."

Pope's very excellence, as I have already had
occasion to say, was an incentive to younger poets
to seek new fields; and they had Pope's encourage-
ment when they proved their competence.   This
side of Pope's relations with his contemporaries has
not yet received the attention which it deserves.
The best of all the poets whom he encouraged was
Thomson.

With the Union of England and Scotland came
the long and endless procession of Scots intent on

finding their livelihood in London or elsewhere in the richer south, and among the early stragglers was James Thomson.   He left Scotland at the age of twenty-five with "a poem in his pocket".   It was his *Winter*.   Within a few years it was to be one of the four parts of *The Seasons*.   He had spent all his youth on the Scottish Border, where his father was a parish minister, or in Edinburgh, where he had himself studied for the ministry at the University.

The traveller who enters Scotland by the Cheviots finds a change in the prospect as he reaches the Border at Carter Bar.   He has been passing through miles and miles of the moorland of Northumberland, but on a sudden he looks down, over a hilly foreground, to a richly wooded and cultivated country, with Jedburgh in the near distance, and further off Hawick and Kelso.   This was Thomson's country.   His early home lay between the rich district to the north and the rough hill country of the Cheviots to the south. The scenery which inspired *The Seasons* was the daily scenery of his youth, viewed through "a kind of glory".   He may refer to many countries, but what he has experienced as a lad is behind what he tells us.   When he writes of frost in winter, and frozen rills, and the death of the shepherd, he is thinking of the Cheviots.   The fishing he describes was in the tributaries of the Tweed.   His agricultural pictures are suggested by farming in the Merse, one of the richest agricultural districts of Scotland. When he speaks of the joys of bathing in summer, he is recollecting through the beautifying mists of memory the warm seasons by the burns of the Jed Water in the parish of Southdean. That *The Seasons* is in origin a poem of the Scottish Border is disguised by the absence of local references and the purposely general description of the great movements of Nature. Sooner than speak of the Border, Thomson will draw imaginary pictures of the Sahara, or Lapland, or the fate of Siberian exiles. Such passages were introduced when his poem became more ambitious, while he was living in the gentler climate of the south of England. But even in them we discover the recollected emotion as, amid the distractions of the great city, he cherishes the memory of his early home.

Nothing in *The Seasons* has given English readers more trouble than the diction. What Pope thought of it is not on record; evidently it did not obscure the merits of the poem for him. But Johnson could not praise it: "His diction is in the highest degree florid and luxuriant. . . . It is too exuberant, and sometimes may be charged with filling the ear more than the mind." Wordsworth is less judicial, and says bluntly that "he writes a vicious style". And I think that all

English purists regard it as a vicious style, pro-
duced in the main by a forced imitation of Milton.
But the English reader is here at a disadvantage.
Thomson was a Scot, and to the educated Scot—
who has always excelled in compiling dictionaries
of the English language, but has not quite the
Englishman's sense of the usage of the words which
he is so proficient in collecting and defining—the
language of *The Seasons* does not offer so great
difficulties.

When Thomson was at the University of
Edinburgh studying for the ministry, he was
reprimanded by the Professor of Divinity for being
too poetically splendid in an exercise on the 119th
Psalm. He was told that "if he thought of being
useful in the ministry he must keep a stricter rein
upon his imagination, and express himself in
language intelligible to an ordinary congregation".
A wholesome censure no doubt, and a common
censure in Scotland. The Scottish student has
always been prone to rhetoric, and his tastes have
been judiciously encouraged. The best English
treatises on rhetoric were produced by Scottish
professors in the eighteenth century. The English
chair at Edinburgh is still called the chair of
"Rhetoric and English Literature"; it used to be
called the chair of "Rhetoric and Belles Lettres".
To the present day the Scottish student dearly
loves a well-rounded resounding sentence. Not so

the English undergraduate. If I may cite my own experience I have never known him rhetorical. His danger is of quite another kind. He may strain after epigram. He likes a crackling style. If when you are rhetorical you run the risk "of filling the ear more than the mind", when you cultivate the epigram there is the risk that your cleverness may miss fire. Both faults are linked to virtues: rhetoric encourages attention to the rhythm of the sentence, and the epigram may conduce to the simple style in which words are not wasted. I believe it is still the experience of a large number of Scots who have followed Thomson and set up their rest in England that they become aware of the need of simplifying their style—of using shorter words now and again, and perhaps fewer words. And again if I may cite my experience, when I return to Scotland and read the leading articles in the newspapers, I get the impression that the vocabulary is slightly heavier than I have become used to in the journalism of the South.

We are apt to forget the large place occupied by Latin in vernacular Scots. Latin was at one time as familiar to the educated Scot as his mother-tongue, and was his means of communication with foreigners. The Scot abroad made his way with Latin. The Scottish authors who were known abroad wrote in Latin. Scots Law, which is founded on Roman Law, has a larger Latin element

than English Law. Latin words were bound to
creep into the vernacular. More than that, Latin
words have come into English from Scottish usage.
An instance is "narrate", which is thus defined by
Johnson in his *Dictionary*—"to relate, to tell; a
word only used in Scotland". Richardson in his
Clarissa has "when I have least to narrate, to speak
in the Scottish phrase, I am most diverting".
Here we have the explanation why the Scottish
historians and philosophers of the eighteenth
century write in a style which seems to the English
reader to be over-Latinized in vocabulary, and, as
our school-masters know, is eminently suitable for
conversion into Latin prose. I have heard a
speaker in one of the debating societies of Edin-
burgh use these words when he wished to express
agreement with what had just been said—
"I homologate the sentiments of the previous
speaker." In Scotland the housewife does not
make tea, she infuses it.

On a style naturally rhetorical, and Latinized,
Thomson superimposed a Miltonic element. He
found in Milton a language after his heart.
"Chimeras huge", "in endless mazes, intricate,
perplexed",—such words and phrases as these
made their way into *The Seasons* much more easily
than we are apt to suppose. *The Seasons* is some-
times spoken of as if it were a long exercise in
aureate diction; but it is too vital a poem for its

language to be a continuous artifice. The style came easily to Thomson; it was natural to him. We can understand why Wordsworth called it vicious, for it is not a style which could have been cultivated by any good English poet. But I should be surprised if, even to-day, it is perplexing to the home-bred Scot. For myself, who may now have to be excluded from that category, I confess that I am attracted by it. Thomson always seems to me to succeed in conveying the impression which he means to convey.

Johnson detected a change of style in the revisions of *The Seasons*. "I know not whether they have not lost part of what Temple calls their *race*; a word which, applied to wines, in its primitive sense, means the flavour of the soil." His observation of the change is only less interesting than his admission of his regret. Thomson's way of writing, like that of other Scots who have left Scotland, was probably modified unconsciously. But after more than twenty years' residence by the banks of the Thames he preserved the Scottish vernacular in his talk. In the brief life written by Robert Shiels, one of Johnson's Scottish assistants on the *Dictionary*, the story is told of a visit paid by an old Edinburgh friend who refused to give his name: "Mr. Thomson came forward to receive him, and looking steadfastly at him (for they had not seen one another for many years) said, 'Troth Sir, I cannot say I ken your countenance well—Let me therefore crave your name'.   Which the gentleman no sooner mentioned but the tears gushed from Mr. Thomson's eyes.   He could only reply, good God! are you the son of my dear friend, my old benefactor; and then rushing to his arms, he tenderly embraced him; rejoicing at so unexpected a meeting."   This is a vivid picture of a sudden access of emotion on remembering happy days, and Thomson's feelings were always easily moved.   We should not be far wrong if we called him the first of the Scottish sentimentalists in English literature. It is sentiment which gives *The Castle of Indolence* its peculiar grace—sentiment which never gets out of control, which is never false or aggressive. Remembrance of Scotland inspires the most famous lines of that poem:

> As when a Shepherd of the *Hebrid-Isles*,
> Plac'd far amid the melancholy Main.

Thomson had seen no more of the Hebrides than of the Sahara or Lapland, but the Hebrides are in Scotland.   The emotional element to be found in all his nature pictures in *The Seasons* is their most characteristic quality.

He begins his *Winter* by describing the delight which as a boy he took in wandering over the hilly country near his home in frost and snow:

> Pleas'd, have I, in my cheerful Morn of Life,
> When, nurs'd by careless *Solitude*, I liv'd,

And sung of Nature with unceasing Joy,
Pleas'd, have I wander'd thro' your rough Domains;
Trod the pure, virgin, Snows, my self as pure:
Heard the Winds roar, and the big Torrent burst:
Or seen the deep, fermenting, Tempest brew'd,
In the red, evening, Sky.—Thus pass'd the Time,
Till, thro' the opening Chambers of the South,
Look'd out the joyous *Spring*, look'd out, and smil'd.[1]

He knows the

> sensations sweet
> Felt in the blood, and felt along the heart,

that are given by the "beauteous forms" of Nature;
but that other gift "of aspect more sublime"
which Wordsworth speaks of in *Tintern Abbey*
Thomson does not reveal. He remains the ob-
server and lover of nature. Her secrets have to
be won from her; she is not an *active* teacher; we
have to draw our own lessons from what she
provides. "I know no subject more elevating,
more amusing", he says, "more ready to awake the
poetical enthusiasm, the philosophical reflection,
and the moral sentiment, than the works of
Nature." He will

> solitary court
> Th' inspiring Breeze; and meditate the Book
> Of Nature, ever open, aiming thence,
> Warm from the Heart, to learn the moral Song.

He meditates the book of Nature. His interests
are partly intellectual, partly moral, and we shall

---

[1]As in the first edition. The edition of 1730 has "the lucid chambers".

agree that what he says comes "warm from the heart".

The emotional bearings of Nature on man are his true theme.   The fault of Pope's early poems, his *Pastorals* and his *Windsor Forest*, was that they were too purely descriptive.   They are accurate in detail, for Pope had lived in the country all his life till he wrote them—and for that matter the Twickenham at which he afterwards lived was still the country by our standards.   But they were written "while pure description held the place of sense".   They do not give us the clue to his own mood.   That was the great lesson which Thomson taught the nature poets of the eighteenth century. Johnson has put it in a memorable sentence: "The reader of *The Seasons* wonders that he never saw before what Thomson shews him, and that he never yet has felt what Thomson impresses."   But of all Thomson's critics I think that Hazlitt is still the best.   Like other Englishmen he did not appreciate Thomson's language, but it could not hide from him the poet.   "Thomson", he says, "is the best of our descriptive poets, for he gives most of the poetry of natural description.   Others have been quite equal to him, or have surpassed him, as Cowper for instance, in the picturesque part of his art, in marking the peculiar features and curious details of objects;—no one has yet come up to him in giving the sum total of their effects, their varying influences on the mind. . . . Nature in his descriptions is seen growing around us, fresh and lusty as in itself. . . . In a word, he describes not to the eye alone, but to the other senses, and to the whole man. He puts his heart into his subject, writes as he feels, and humanises whatever he touches." High praise, and the more remarkable as it was written when Hazlitt was familiar with the poetry of Wordsworth. But Wordsworth is not primarily a descriptive poet. He has an unsurpassed power of suggesting a scene in a few words, but he soon takes us far beyond it. The art of Thomson remains purposely pictorial; and this is true of the best nature poetry of the century.

Treating Nature pictorially, he presents it as a background to human activity, the scene on which man has his being. It was more than a background to Wordsworth. But I would suggest that it is not more than a background to most of us, and that even among Wordsworth's most ardent admirers there are few who can bring themselves to think of it habitually, or for any length of time, as he did.

The Seasons won immediate popularity. No one attacked it, no one considered its novelty to be rebellious. It went into many editions, each one of which Thomson carefully revised and augmented; the final edition of the four parts is some fifteen hundred lines longer than the first.

Its popularity continued till well into the nine-
teenth century. I have known a house—it was
in Scotland—where a well-bound copy lay on the
drawing-room table.

The language of Burns, unlike that of Thomson,
does not seem to have detracted from his apprecia-
tion by English readers. They may have difficulty
in understanding it, but they never mistake it for
"vicious" English. They accept its strange idiom,
and, in company with a large number of Scottish
enthusiasts, make the best of it.

In one sense Burns was less original than
Thomson. He did not have a new subject, or a
new manner. He began by imitation, and to the
end of his life his ambition was to excel within the
tradition. His originality consists in doing better
than his Scottish predecessors what they had done.
He is content with what he finds, knowing what
he can make of it. What generations of Scots had
been saying, or trying to say, finds in him its
rememberable expression.

We are not to think that Burns's mastery of
the craft of words came to him without long
practice, nor to forget the old proverb that Heaven
helps them who help themselves. In a brave
moment he had affected to despise book-learning
and had proclaimed the sufficiency of his un-
tutored gifts:

> Gie me ae spark o' Nature's fire,
> That's a' the learning I desire.

He had been given this spark of Nature's fire, but
no one knew better than he did that he had to
learn how to make use of it. "Excellence in the
profession", he says in a letter written after he
had come to his fame, "is the fruit of industry,
labour, attention, and pains"; and there he is
talking seriously. From the days when he first
had the ambition to write poems of his own he
had studied the poems of others.

In a long autobiographical letter he included a
full account of his early reading: "My knowledge
of ancient story was gathered from Salmon's and
Guthrie's geographical grammars; my knowledge
of modern manners, and of literature and criticism,
I got from the Spectator.—These, with Pope's
works, some plays of Shakespear, Tull and Dick-
son on Agriculture, The Pantheon, Locke's Essay
on the human understanding, Stackhouse's history
of the bible, Justice's British Gardiner's directory,
Boyle's lectures, Allan Ramsay's works, Taylor's
scripture doctrine of original sin, a select Collection
of English songs, and Hervey's meditations had
been the extent of my reading." In this remark-
able list only Allan Ramsay's works are in the
Scottish vernacular; and Burns goes on to show
that they were of much less importance to him than
the "select Collection of English songs". "The

Collection of Songs was my vade mecum.—I pored over them, driving my cart or walking to labor, song by song, verse by verse; carefully noting the true tender or sublime from affectation and fustian.— I am convinced I owe much to this for my critic-craft such as it is." This Collection has not been convincingly identified; but we have to note that it contained English songs, not Scottish. "My reading", he continues, "was enlarged with the very important addition of Thomson's and Shenstone's works. . . . I had met with a collection of letters by the Wits of Queen Ann's reign, and I pored over them most devoutly. . . . The addition of two more Authors to my library gave me great pleasure; Sterne and McKenzie. Tristram Shandy and the Man of Feeling were my bosom favorites." Still later he read stray volumes of Richardson's *Pamela* and Smollett's *Count Fathom*.

Burns gave himself an English training. From this account it appears that his reading was mainly in the English literature of his own century, though he also read Shakespeare and Milton. What he thus learned about the art of writing he was to turn to account in his Scottish poems. The crisis in his career came at the age of twenty-three, when he read the poems of Robert Fergusson, and was moved to follow their example. Fergusson, a lawyer's clerk in Edinburgh, had drawn pictures of the life of the capital in the vernacular as it was there spoken, and in traditional Scottish measures. What Fergusson had done for Edinburgh, Burns was to do for his Ayrshire. A few years later at the age of twenty-seven, he brought out the famous Kilmarnock edition.

A comparison of this edition with Fergusson's *Scots Poems* shows almost at a glance how closely it is imitative. Burns has not an easier command of the language, nor has he a more caustic wit, but he excels in his greater range of mood and in his fuller sense of the joy of life. Fergusson had recently died insane; and much of the attraction of the Kilmarnock volume lies in the impression which it gives us of sheer health. But Fergusson had revealed to Burns the possibilities of their native tongue, and Burns never forgot his debt to

my elder brother in misfortune,
By far my elder brother in the Muse.

With the publication of the Kilmarnock volume the unknown Ayrshire farmer, who held the plough and himself worked his land, leapt to fame with a bound. And no wonder. It was a remarkable volume that opened with *The Twa Dogs* and contained *The Holy Fair*, the *Address to the Deil*, *Halloween*, *The Cotter's Saturday Night*, the poems *To a Mouse* and *To a Mountain-Daisy*, besides some of his very best epistles to his friends,—a kind of epistle in which he has no rival. But the volume did not contain one song that is generally

known.   Burns made his name by poems which
were descriptive of Scottish life and gave oppor-
tunities for a mingled display of wit, and satire,
and sentiment; and there was nothing novel in
them beyond their excellence.

Most of us read Burns in collected editions, or
in selections, but we had better try to see the
Kilmarnock edition as it appeared should we want
to understand the effect which it produced.   If
none of the twenty-four original copies which are
known to survive should be available, we can
always handle to our heart's content a facsimile or
reprint.   We may be struck by the absence of
songs, but nothing will strike us more than the
number of well-known pieces or familiar passages
which crowd upon each other as we turn its pages.

The new edition of his poems which was brought
out the next year at Edinburgh—whither his fame
had taken him away from his Ayrshire farm—
contains new pieces of the same kind, *Death and
Dr. Hornbook*, *The Brigs of Ayr*, and *Address to the
Unco Guid*, and only a few songs, the best known
of which are *John Barleycorn* and *Green Grow the
Rashes*.   It did not contain *The Jolly Beggars* and
other songs which had been written in Ayrshire
and might have been included.   In the choice of
his poems Burns was still influenced by the example
of Fergusson, and only his intimate friends would
think of him as a song-writer.

While he was in Edinburgh he became acquainted with the music engraver who was producing *The Scots Musical Museum*. This engraver, James Johnson by name, could attend to the music, but he asked for help with the words; and from this time to the end of his life Burns's main occupation as a poet was the refurbishing of old songs, and the writing of new songs to old airs. Some of the songs which he had already written he was now to publish; and he was not to confine himself to songs,—he was still to write, for example, *Tam o' Shanter*. But henceforward he was to be, pre-eminently, a song-writer. He was to be the great song-writer of Scotland, and one of the greatest song-writers of the world.

Altogether he wrote or rewrote between three hundred and four hundred songs. The great example of his rewriting is *Auld Lang Syne*. In a primitive form it is as old as the seventeenth century, and it had been twice doctored editorially, first in James Watson's *Choice Collection of Scots Poems* in 1711, and again by Allan Ramsay for his *Tea-Table Miscellany* in 1724. Had the poem survived only in the version of Watson or Ramsay, it would itself have been "forgot and never brought to mind". Instead it is the parting song of good fellowship not only in Scotland, but in England, and, I understand, wherever English is spoken. (How many know the meaning of all the words,

how many Scots can repeat it correctly, need not
be enquired.)   In the difficult art of preserving the
floating fragments of national song, Burns, for all
I know, may have his equal in some other country,
but I cannot believe that he has ever been sur-
passed.   No praise can be too high for his mastery
in giving new life to the remnants of an old tradi-
tion.   We may wonder what would have become
of Scottish song without Burns.

He is no less within the tradition in his own
Scottish songs.   There, too, he had no thought of
reform; he had no attack to make on convention;
his function was to carry on.   He took lessons
from the English poets, but only when he is con-
scious of his Scottish inheritance does he write
with ease and conviction.   "I think my ideas are
more barren in English than in Scotish", he said.
And again, "Are you not quite vexed to think that
these men of genius, for such they certainly were,
who composed our fine Scotish lyrics, should be
unknown?   It has given me many a heart-ach."
In that spirit he became their successor.

Burns generally wrote his songs to a tune.
"To sough [*i.e.*, hum] the tune over and over", he
says, "is the readiest way to catch the inspiration
and raise the Bard into that glorious enthusiasm
so strongly characteristic of our old Scotch poetry."
He has described his method even minutely:

"Untill I am compleat master of a tune, in my own singing, (such as it is) I never can compose for it.— My way is: I consider the poetic Sentiment, correspondent to my idea of the musical expression; then chuse my theme; begin one Stanza; when that is composed, which is generally the most difficult part of the business, I walk out, sit down now and then, look out for objects in Nature around me that are in unison or harmony with the cogitations of my fancy and workings of my bosom; humming every now and then the air with the verses I have framed: when I feel my Muse beginning to jade, I retire to the solitary fireside of my study, and there commit my effusions to paper; swinging, at intervals, on the hind-legs of my elbow-chair, by way of calling forth my own critical strictures, as my pen goes on.—Seriously, this, at home, is almost invariably my way.—What damn'd Egotism!"

He made no claims for himself as a musician. "You know", he writes, "that my pretensions to musical taste, are merely a few of Nature's instincts, untaught and untutored by Art.—For this reason, many musical compositions, particularly where much of the merit lies in Counterpoint, however they may transport and ravish the ears of you, Connoisseurs, affect my simple lug no otherwise than merely as melodious Din.—On the other hand, by way of amends, I am delighted with many little melodies, which the learned Musician despises as silly and insipid." And he goes on to tell how he composed *Scots Wha Hae* to an old air.

These airs were the old Scottish airs, traditional airs; and by composing to them Burns preserved the tradition in his original compositions,—he re-produced it in his own medium, the medium of words. What was this tradition but the genius of the people expressing itself from generation to generation in the way in which it could express itself best? In the poetry of Burns it found clear and unwavering voice. The traditional element in his work has contributed to make him the national poet of Scotland, more incontestably than any poet is the national poet of England.

It may be doubted if England, with all her un-matched wealth of poetry, has a national poet. Even Shakespeare is too great, too individual, too much by himself, to be accepted as speaking for his fellow-men. Not so Burns. He is never beyond their capacity. He does not speak to them so much as for them; and he could have had no higher ambition. There was much in Scottish life at this time against which, in common with many others, he rebelled, but there was nothing to be overthrown in Scottish poetry. He kept to the old subjects, the old measures, and the old manner, and was original in the mastery with which he used them.

If in view of Burns's world-wide reputation I

should seem to you to have laid too great stress on the national qualities of his verse, I would plead that my intention has been to give due prominence to his historical position, and thus to view him clearly in his relation to the great revival of poetry that came in England with the nineteenth century. Burns perfected the Scottish tradition in poetry at a time when English poetry was passing through one of its poorer periods, when, as Blake lamented, the sounds were forced, the notes were few. In the pages of Burns Scottish poetry was brought to the notice of English readers. They mistook him for a reformer, they looked upon him as a herald of a new age, because they found in him the lost charm of spontaneous song. But a long history lies behind his work, and much discipline had gone to its making. No wonder that they hailed him as a great original genius, as indeed he was. But Burns was a true child of the Scottish eighteenth century.

Let us not forget, however, that England has her own songs in the eighteenth century. She did not excel then in love songs, but she gave us songs that we all know, and though we may not think of them as outstanding works of poetical art, we should be sorry to be without them. The great lyrical utterances come from the heart of man in solitude, when he is driven in upon himself and must speak. Are not love songs usually inspired by regrets at one's solitude? As I have already remarked, the century may strike us as being a little too grown-up to indulge in pining for what is not. But it was an eminently social century, and it gave us songs that are sung in unison, songs with a chorus, songs for jovial companies or for crowds. It gave us *God Save the King*, which dates from about 1745 but did not become the national anthem till many years later. It gave us *Rule Britannia* about the same time, in 1740. It gave us *Heart of Oak* and *The British Grenadiers*. It gave us *A Hunting We Will Go*, and *The Roast Beef of Old England*, and *Tom Bowling*. These are social songs,—songs for men in the company of their fellows.

And it gave us most of our best hymns. This is the century of Isaac Watts, the Wesleys, and Cowper.

It is now time for me to conclude and to retire from office as your Alexander lecturer. I may perhaps seem to some of you to have been too much inclined, while speaking of the tradition in English poetry, to break away from what has now been for two or three generations the tradition in English criticism. I sometimes think we should get a truer view of the poetry of this century if we could rediscover it for ourselves and forget all that the critics have said about it. The more I read it, the more I feel that it has much to tell us in these days. In its great variety I do not find any conflict. The different strands combine in a pattern, which, as I see it, represents the English genius at one of its most characteristic stages.   There are many moods in which we turn to this poetry, and in each of them it yields a satisfaction which we cannot easily find elsewhere.